MONSTERS
ON THE MOVE

Timothy Kane

TRIUMPH
B O O K S

This book is available in quantity at special discounts for your group or
organization. For further information, contact:

Triumph Books LLC
542 South Dearborn Street
Suite 750
Chicago, Illinois 60605
(312) 939-3330
Fax (312) 663-3557
www.triumphbooks.com

Printed in U.S.A.

ISBN: 978-1-60078-716-4

Content developed and packaged by Rockett Media, Inc.
Writer: Timothy Kane
Editor: Bob Baker
Design and page production: Andrew Burwell
All photos courtesy of Getty Images & AP Photos unless otherwise noted.

MONSTERS ON THE MOVE

WEIRD STREET

Y ou better put in your earplugs. The show is about to start. It gets loud in here.

You are sitting in your seat, with a bag of chips and a jumbo lemonade on your lap. The show is about to begin.

All of a sudden — bam! Is it an explosion? The whole building is shaking. Is it an earthquake?

Perhaps the stadium is on top of a fault line. It feels like 7.0 on the Richter scale.

Hold on to your seat. The place is getting shakier. The roar is getting louder.

What could it be?

You and the other spectators are looking around, trying to figure out what's happening.

Maybe the space shuttle landed on the roof of the stadium by mistake.

You are wondering what the heck can be causing the racket.

Zounds!

Emerging from a dark tunnel under the grandstands is a revved-up, roaring

Monster Truck. The front end of the monster emerges slowly from the shadows. Then, the full snorting beast shoots out from the tunnel at what seems like a zillion miles per hour, spewing fire from its exhaust pipes.

A blue haze settles up in the rafters, like the roof is on fire. You want to cover your face from the noise and the smoke. You are scared, but you don't want to admit it.

Did your parents tell you that you were coming to Weird Street? It's the place where monsters roam free. You're in the freak zone. Flying shrapnel, the debris from colliding

and exploding monsters, can be dangerous. Be prepared to duck. Hide behind the seat in front of you, if you can.

Meanwhile, as you cower and shiver, the beast with giant wheels keeps snorting and tearing the place to pieces. It drives insanely around in circles and jumps over hills of dirt and runs over the top of junkyard relics. The Monster Truck's giant tires spin and shoot dirt clods through the air like muddy fireworks.

You are scared, terrified, shaking. You are more frightened than you ever have been before. This is worse than the first time you went through a carwash.

However, the joke's on you. Your parents' cell-phone camera has captured all of your excitement on video. Your public spasm at your first Monster Truck show is now a hit on YouTube.

WEIRDEST OF THE WEIRD

Where else can trucks with humongous wheels run over cars and crush them flat, just for the fun of it?

It happens only here on Weird Street.

Weirdos on parade include monsters that look like large beasts. Some look like mutant lizards, dripping primordial ooze.

One weirdo looks like a big-eared puppy, with a tongue sticking out from the engine compartment.

Another weirdo calls itself the Batmobile. … Yeah, right, maybe it's the Batmobile on steroids.

How about a monster ice cream truck? It'll bust loose every so often, coming to a neighborhood near you.

Imagine spotting an ice cream truck with giant wheels on the street where you live, circling your block, playing that annoying music. The monster ice cream truck is about six times bigger than any car on your street. The driver sits up high and the kids are down low, running down the sidewalk, screaming: "Ice cream! Ice cream! Ice cream!"

The driver stomps on the brakes. The monster screeches to a halt at the end of a 50-foot skid mark.

"What do you want kid," he'll ask. "A Popsicle? A frozen double-dip twinkle bar?"

Be warned. You can't pay this guy with lint balls and loose nickels. This guy only trades in bent hubcaps and hood ornaments, pried loose from flattened wrecks.

Last, but not least, the weirdest of them all is the monster school bus. Can you imagine needing a ladder to get on the bus? Imagine that today is your birthday. The bus driver knows it.

"What's your birthday wish, kid?" the bus driver asks. "Name it. I can make it happen."

You say, "Flatten all the cars in the teachers' parking lot. Spare the janitor. I like that guy."

"You got it, kid," the bus driver says as the crunch begins.

Remember, kid, this stuff doesn't just happen in your imagination … it happens on Weird Street.

THE BIRTH OF BIGFOOT

Who is Bob Chandler? He is the man who many say invented the Monster Truck. He is a real-life legend. Almost 40 years ago, back in 1975, Bob wanted to show off his new ride, a 1975 F-150 Ford pickup. He was proud of it and wanted others to share his enthusiasm.

He wanted people to notice his truck when he was driving to work, or to the supermarket, or to the gas station. However, Bob found that it was hard to get attention because the F-series Ford was one of the

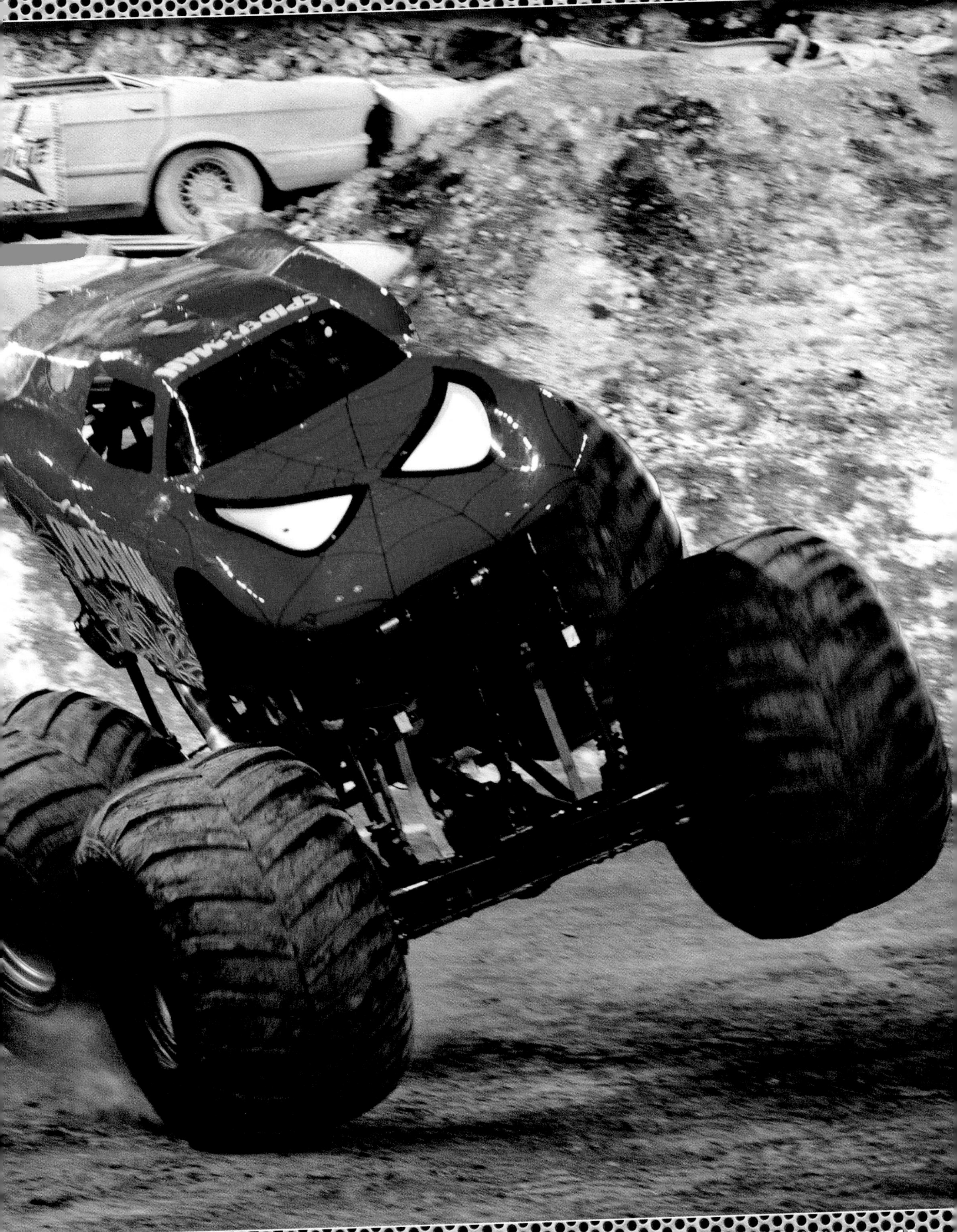

most popular automobiles on the street. (About 1 million of these vehicles are manufactured every year, according to the *Guinness Book of World Records*.) Bob had his work cut out for him. He wanted people to notice him, but he was driving one of the most commonly seen vehicles on the road. To get anyone's attention would require extreme measures. He figured the best way to change things was to make his truck look as weird as possible, weirder than any other truck out on the street.

In an interview Bob gave to a reporter from the *Arizona Republic* newspaper, he said he never intended on making a monster … it just happened.

"I just kept putting parts onto my truck," Bob told the reporter. "It was a vicious circle. I put on bigger tires, so I needed a bigger axle. The tires were difficult to turn, so we came up with rear-wheel steering. … Then I needed a bigger engine."

Bob said it took four years to fully complete the job. Now we know why it's called a Monster Truck. The Frankenstein monster was put together the same way — piece by piece.

Bob Chandler is also recognized as being the first individual to use his Monster Truck to crush a car. He named his first truck Bigfoot and used it to flatten a car in the spring of 1981. You can watch the historic event on YouTube. This one event has led to all of the interesting escapades you can see nowadays on the Weird Street stage.

CREATURE FEATURES

Weird Street has its contenders for strangest vehicle. They all have unique qualities that make each one special. You don't have to be fluent in Spanish to know what El Toro Loco means. In English it means "The Crazy Bull." El Toro Loco is a Monster Truck that has horns like

a bull. Sometimes it faces a monster called El Matador. Despite their names. they don't do battle in a bullring. Instead, they race one another onstage. El Toro Loco has won one world championship and has been on the Monster Jam circuit since 2003.

Have you heard of Monster Mutt? This weird canine vehicle is like a cross between Snoopy and Godzilla. It has floppy doggy ears, a floppy doggy tail, and a doggy tongue stinking out from under its hood, hanging over the top of the radiator. But don't let these puppy features calm your fears. This is a Monster Mutt. You know not to throw it a bone or play fetch with it. Just run for your life.

Another creature turned into a Monster Truck is Swamp Thing. This creature spawned from the comic books is kind of gross, with green skin covered in damp green seaweed and slimy green algae. The comic-book character Swamp Thing is a mad scientist caught in one of his experiments. The Monster Truck Swamp Thing is actually not so hideous. It is painted a revolting green, and it has "Swamp Thing" written across all its sides.

There's another truck that fell out of the ugly tree and hit every branch on the way down. Jurassic Attack is the name of the Monster Truck triceratops. It's a four-wheeled dinosaur that has all of the features of a triceratops: two horns sticking

out above the eyebrows and one horn sticking out of the nose. It also has dappled aquamarine skin and its eyes are set wide apart — one on the driver-side window and the other on the passenger-side window. In addition, it has a white beak instead of an upper lip. Good thing Weird Street is a place for racing and not for beauty contests.

TWO KINDS OF MONSTERS

As you have learned in school, mammals are not the same as reptiles. One difference is that a mammal has hair and a reptile doesn't.

It's the same with the famous Monster Trucks you see on the Weird Street stage compared to the homegrown Monsters you see driving around the neighborhood. Sometimes it's hard to tell, but they are definitely two different animals.

One big difference is the showbiz Monsters were designed and built from scratch. They were manufactured to be Monster Trucks from the beginning.

The old-school Monsters you might see tooling through town were once just normal-looking Jeeps or pickups that were hacked up and rebuilt with bigger pieces. Sort of like greasy Dr. Frankensteins going out looking for parts to build their monster.

In the evolution of Monster Trucks, the original Monsters were homemade. The first mad scientists were enthusiastic mechanics who started

putting tractor tires on their cars and trucks.

(A cousin of the Monster Truck, by the way, is the dune buggy.)

Once they started tinkering, they couldn't stop. When they added bigger tires, it meant bigger suspension systems. It also meant providing more torque to turn the wheels, which required bigger axles and bigger drive shafts. This resulted in the need for more power, which could only be supplied by bigger engines. The engines needed to be so large, in fact, the drivers had to cut holes in the hood, making it easier for the carburetor to suck air.

Finally, these mechanics started putting on shows in cornfields, crushing junkyard relics, and giving their Monsters weird names and fancy paint jobs. The old Monster Trucks were all covered in dried mud. The mud operated as a badge of honor. The driver of the Monster wanted everyone to know that he really had been down and dirty with his truck. It was important to document that he'd been toilet papered. It was important to document that he drove into a pit of mud and survived.

A big plus for the old-school Monster is that it was a family vehicle. If your Monster was a pickup, there was plenty of room for suitcases. You could take it on vacation and bring the whole family — or whoever fit. A good vacation for the original Monsters was a mud pit, dirt hill, a swamp or a bog … anything to wallow in. Running over cars can get expensive. You don't see that happening too much out on the streets. The stage show is left for the famous Monsters appearing onstage at a stadium near you.

You have to feel a little sorry for the Hollywood Monsters who only appear at a show and not on the road. They are so big, they'd hog the road and leave no room for anyone else. The cops won't let them drive down your street. They lead the tortured lives of real-life monsters. They barely ever see the light of day. They are brought to the shows inside a coffin-like crate, inside the back of a semi. Most showbiz Monsters only have a seat for one driver and no one else. Once they are set free, they behave just like any old monster. They are stir crazy. It's no wonder when they're let loose, they tear around the arena, driving in crazy circles and making their own dust storm. The only time they get to rev their engines and run wild is at the shows on Weird Street.

WORLDWIDE POPULARITY FOR MONSTERS

Imagine 10,000 Monster fans singing "Happy Birthday"… in Polish.

At a recent show in Europe, a crowd of monster fans sang a version of "Happy Birth-

FUN FACT

Weight lifters often use Monster Truck tires for what is called a "caveman workout." They put the tires in the gym, next to the dumbbells. The strong man, when working out, picks up the tire and turns it over like you would a pancake. There are bodybuilding websites that give demonstrations on how to flip a monster tire. Where do you find a gigantic old tire to do a tire-flipping workout? You may want to ask a farmer if he's got any spares in the barn.

day to You" in their native tongue. Can you imagine the noise? The target of this sing-along was Charles Benns, the driver of the Monster Mutt Rottweiler. Benns and his beast were on a world tour when the birthday celebration erupted on Weird Street, according to the Monster Jam website.

A love for Monster Trucks seems to cross all barriers. It doesn't take a common language to figure out what's happening with Monster Trucks. International admirers love the thrills, chills, and mayhem. They express their shared enthusiasm in many different languages.

Monster Jam's International Tour in 2011 included Helsinki, Finland; Barcelona, Spain; and Monterrey, Mexico. Other parts of Europe, Asia, and South America also had similar shows with different promoters, owners, and competitors.

Why do so many people from so many different countries like Monster Trucks?

"Monster Jam is an exercise in the appreciation of man's mechanical achievements by way of customized Monster Truck(s)," writes Sam Williams, a contributor to the eHow website.

He said this is a common appreciation that fans share all over the world. "Trucks race one another to see who is the fastest, while performing stunts such as leaping off ramps," Williams says. As with any sport, he said fans pick and cheer for their favorites, such as Grave Digger and Maximum Destruction, no matter where they are from.

BIG WHEELS

hat makes a Monster Truck a monster? The answer is big wheels!

Street monsters use tires made for farm tractors and other kinds of construction equipment. These wheels need to be big, because they provide the torque and traction necessary to do the heavy lifting on the side of the road. It's the tires that do the grunt work, moving the dirt and rocks.

When it comes to the showbiz monsters, they get special tire treatment. Goodyear and Firestone manufacture custom-made tires that are 66 inches tall. To understand the size of these wheels, divide 66 inches by 12 — as in 12 inches per foot — which comes to 5½ feet. This means the tires on a showbiz monster are almost as tall as your parents. Wow!

An offspring of Bob Chandler's original monster is named Bigfoot V. It has tires almost twice as tall as the average monster, about 10 feet tall, or as tall as a grizzly bear standing up on its hind legs. Bigfoot V was named the world's biggest pickup truck by the Guinness Book of World Records. Chandler got the 10-foot tires from the U.S. Army, which had been using these humongous wheels for off-road adventures in Alaska.

MONSTER HALL-OF-FAME INDUCTEES

He didn't want to do it at first. Bob Chandler confessed that he thought that people wouldn't like if he crushed cars in front of an audience.

MOST POPULAR STUNTS IN ANY LANGUAGE

Performing monsters execute live stunts such as driving in crazy circles called "donuts." They jump ramps and sail through the air, which is called "going airborne." They also get up on their rear tires — like a dog on its hind legs begging for a chewy snack — and do wheelies, which are called "tail stands." According to eHow contributor Timothy Burns, the most dangerous stunt is called the "two-wheel turn." This is done when the monster driver is "burning donuts" and then "makes a sharp turn, causing the inner wheels come off the ground." At times, a two-wheel turn may cause a monster to self-destruct, breaking into pieces that go flying through the air.

Duck!

FUN FACT

Many Monster Trucks are buoyant … in other words they float like a boat because of their big tires. You can watch floating monsters on YouTube. When their tires are spinning, moving them forward, they resemble paddleboats.

He feared that people would think that it was wanton destruction, wasteful, moronic, frivolous tomfoolery … a dumb lark … and so on.

But Chandler was wrong, and now, decades later, he is one of the first inductees into the International Monster Truck Museum & Hall of Fame. Chandler is credited with revolutionizing the pastime of flattening cars by running them over.

It all started not far from his home in Missouri. Chandler used a big-wheeled Ford pickup to crush two cars parked on a stretch of farmland one day. He captured this novel activity on video and a new sport was born. You can view this original video on YouTube.

Chandler took his video of the car crushing to a show promoter, who recognized the appeal of this unusual hobby. He asked Chandler to crush cars in front of a paying audience. Chandler, though, in an online interview, said at first he was hesitant to bring his

new hobby to the stage. He thought that the people who wanted to watch a tractor pull would find a car crush offensive.

Chandler said he finally gave in and crushed a few cars at a big show at the Pontiac Silverdome. The crowd loved it, he said. They went wild. They wanted to see the demolition of these junkyard relics. The crowd was thirsty for more motor oil.

"People like destruction," Chandler told an interviewer from *Truck Show TV*. "The truck got to be the star. After that, we had to crush cars everywhere we went."

Early on, Chandler wondered how long the appeal of car crushing would last. Now, nearly 40 years later, he sees no end in sight.

Chandler, founder and owner of the Bigfoot Monster Truck empire based in a suburb of St. Louis, is credited with being the first gearhead to put gigantic tires on a vehicle.

The Monster Truck Hall of Famer said that he put on bigger tires than anybody else because he wanted to go places nobody else could go. And he wanted to be noticed.

Chandler said his vehicle was simply known as "Bigfoot" back when it was first unveiled. Chandler credits big-event announcer Bob Jones — at a show at the Pontiac Silverdome — with thinking up the term "Monster Truck." … And the rest is history.

FUN FACT
Auburn, Indiana, is the hometown of Gordon Buehrig
[1904-1990] designer of the 1935-1936 Auburn Speedster.

Others along with Chandler being induct-
ed as the original class into the Hall of Fame
include Dan Degrasso, Jeff Dane, Everett
Jasmer, Fred Shafer, and Jack Willman Sr. The
first induction ceremony was held Novem-
ber 19, 2011, at the International Monster
Truck Museum & Hall of Fame in Auburn,
Indiana.

SPOOKY MONSTER TRUCK

About four years ago, a mysterious
guy bought Brutte Boss Hogg, a
Monster Truck. After he paid for it, he
never took it home with him. He disappeared.

The guy was an out-of-towner and paid
$35,000 for the monster to the Grams family,
owners of the Volo Auto Museum in the north-
west suburbs of Chicago.

"He just disappeared," Brian Grams said.
"It's like he fell off the face of the earth."

Myra Grams, Brian's mother, said the
stranger had bought expensive antique cars
from them before. However, in the past, he
had always taken his purchases home with
him, but not this time.

His purchase — Brutte Boss Hogg — is
not just an old-school Monster Truck; it is
said to be one of the originals. It's one of the
prototypes, made into a Monster Truck even
before Bob Chandler's Bigfoot.

Brutte Boss Hogg was built by a gearhead by the name of Randy Weber.

This monster was named after a character on a popular television show called "The Dukes of Hazzard." The Boss Hogg character was the county sheriff in the show.

Brutte Boss Hogg now sits alone near the back fence of the Volo Museum property in the sleepy hamlet of Volo, Illinois. The Gans family had sold it and taken the money, they didn't own it any longer. Myra Grams said she's not sure what to do with it now. She's been waiting years and still the buyer hasn't arrived to take his monster home.

When they were owners of Brutte Boss Hogg, the Grams family did all the normal things that one does with a Monster Truck. They put on shows and ran over junk cars with it. And, in the fall, they ran over pumpkins with it.

Now, it sits alone, waiting to be claimed. It's a mystery, still waiting to be solved …

MILITARY MONSTERS

We're going to talk about a new breed of blast-proof Monster Trucks — made by the Oshkosh Corporation — that are being used by the U.S. Army and the U.S. Marine Corps. These are used to maneuver in hostile regions, on primitive roads, and over boulder-strewn landscapes, all while in the crosshairs of enemy snipers.

Let me introduce you to the M-ATV — the U.S. Defense Department's All-Terrain Vehicle. This battle-proven monster can take a bullet like a spitball. All branches of the military are using the M-ATV. This vehicle can morph from an ambu-

lance into a combat vehicle fitted with machine guns and rocket launchers. Or it can be fitted with radio-jamming equipment that will turn an enemy's radio transmissions into garbled gobbledygook. The M-ATV is tough. It was designed to withstand a powerful blast and keep U.S. soldiers safe. It can withstand roadside bombs and every kind of mine, missile, and booby-trap.

One account of a Taliban attack on an M-ATV in Afghanistan was reported on the General Motors forum like this:

"The Taliban had them surrounded. It was a clear, moonlit night on March 28, 2010, in Dangam district, in the Kunar River Valley in eastern Afghanistan. A U.S. Army patrol was caught on a narrow road between two mountain peaks teeming with Taliban fighters.

'They hit us from both sides,' first lieutenant Cris Gasperini, the patrol leader, recalled a few days after the battle.

Rocket-propelled grenades were launched from the mountain peaks. In quick succession, three rockets struck one of the vehicles in the patrol, an M-ATV — each projectile exploding with a blinding flash and a thunderclap that left ears ringing. The Taliban fighters might have imagined, for a moment, that they had scored a major victory against the Americans. However, when the noise and light had faded, the only in-dication that the vehicle had been hit was a few dents and streaks of soot."

WHAT'S IT REALLY LIKE BACKSTAGE?

Not many wannabe daredevils get a chance to drive an actual showbiz monster. It's a specialized machine and it takes years of practice to get it right. Monster Jam's Dennis Anderson takes out a monster for a few freestyle laps. When he's ready to take off, a member of his pit crew tells him through a walkie-talkie "all systems are ready," just like a launch into outer space.

Anderson is driving Grave Digger. The monster is rigged with remote video cameras inside the cockpit and mounted underneath the chassis. One camera has a stomach-churning view of a spinning driveshaft. Monster-driver Anderson is dressed like a fighter pilot, complete with a crash

helmet and a one-piece jumpsuit. He's also strapped into his seat.

When you conquer a monster, you'll see that Anderson drives solo, all by himself. There is only room for one person in the one seat in front of the steering wheel of this monster. He zips around the dirt hills and runs over junkyard clunkers. Inside, from the camera's view, you can see he must be getting dizzy. It's like a ride in a blender, being turned into a milkshake. But he's got to keep his wits. The show must go on!

You'll see the Grave Digger get launched into the air, after driving off the end of a dirt ramp. There follows a second or two of calmness, then boom! Grave Digger bounces off the dirt track and is airborne again for another second or two, before it bounces off the dirt track again. The showbiz monster's fiberglass skin sometimes breaks into a thousand pieces during the performance … just another day on the Monster Truck stage.

The monster suspension and shock absorbers may take a lot of the pounding, but not all of it. The drivers need to be equally tough.

INCREDIBLE SHRINKING MONSTERS

You don't see the really big monsters anymore … at least not driving around your neighborhood. You can only find the giant monsters onstage.

Ted Smak has been making street monsters since about 1985. His monster laboratory is not in Transylvania. He's got a shop in America where he jacks up pickup trucks and fits them with bigger wheels and roll bars. He said the Monster Trucks he's making nowadays have smaller tires than when he started out. He can't really build them big anymore. It's the law.

People were frightened by the size of monsters they were seeing. They didn't want them driving down highways and streets used by regular cars and trucks. Perhaps the public was afraid the monsters would run amok and start flattening your Uncle Chuck's Cadillac or your Aunt Tillie's Volkswagen Bug.

Most states have limited the height of monsters to 27 inches from the ground to the front bumper and 29 inches from the ground to the back bumper. That's only a midget monster compared to the showbiz vehicles you see on the big stage. The street monsters are barely scary.

You better watch out if your street monster is bigger than the law allows. Police in many states will impound a monster that is too big. A mon-

ster with giant wheels is like a crazy dog that has to be put behind bars.

"Nowadays to get a big monster to a mud hole, you have to take off the wheels and put the monster — minus the wheels because it won't fit in a semi — and drive it to the mud hole," Smak said. "Then you have to put the wheels back on after you get there. Some people think it's too much trouble and they've stopped going to mud holes. It's a shame."

Smak has driven many monsters, and nearly all of them were his own creation. He takes them out for test drives after he has finished jacking them up.

One time he drove a really big showbiz Monster Truck. Its name was First Blood. And he said it was one of the biggest thrills of his life.

His most cherished monster is Big Iron, a monster-converted 1979 Ford F-150. It made the cover of a popular off-road magazine in the early 1980s, Smak said. It has a chrome bulldog for a hood ornament, made for a Mack Truck. He pampers Big Iron like a baby. Smak said he doesn't want his monster to get cold or get caught outside in the snow.

"It has spent only one winter outside," Smak said.

Years ago, he didn't have room for Big Iron in his garage. Instead, he built a shed especially for it by parking it on the side of his house and nailing boards together around it. Nowadays, his famous monster gets special treatment. He keeps it inside the garage. It's been there since 1983.

Smak said Big Iron is currently missing a battery and other parts. But he said he's determined to bring it back to life and let it roam. He's going to fix it up one of these days.